Down *to* Earth

This is dedicated to the women who served in the Women's Land Army.

Down *to* Earth

Memories of a young woman joining the Women's Land Army in 1943

Nancy Cooper

BREWIN BOOKS

First published by
Brewin Books Ltd, 56 Alcester Road,
Studley, Warwickshire B80 7LG in 2017
www.brewinbooks.com

ISBN: 978-1-85858-572-7

A Cataloguing in Publication Record
for this title is available from the British Library.

Typeset in Haarlemmer MT Std.
Printed in Great Britain by
Hobbs The Printers Ltd.

Contents

Acknowledgements

This book would not have been written without the help of Marilyn Burrill who guided me, made all the arrangements with the publisher and did all the typing. My grateful thanks.

Foreword

I always had a great affection for animals and was very interested in nature. At school I didn't seem to make any progress and had very little confidence. War was declared just before my fourteenth birthday and life completely changed.

I left school at fourteen and in September 1939 we were suddenly plunged into wartime conditions. Blacked out with no street lights, rationing food, clothes and household furniture. Gas masks, evacuees so it goes on. Women had to work or were recruited into the forces which included the Land Army. I joined as soon as I was of age.

We didn't get much recognition, a badge after 58 years in 2008 and a sculpture after 64 years. However, I am proud of the beautiful statue. Now at long last the workers who made the ammunition, especially the ones that did a very dangerous side of it, have been recognised. It is well deserved and should have happened long ago.

So many people I have talked to don't know anything about wartime conditions or the Land Army. However, the war brought comradeship, a togetherness and especially helping each other. Something we have lost, in many cases it has caused much loneliness, especially with my age group.

By this personal message I wish to express to you

Miss Nancy Edna WALKER.
W.L.A. No: 120220.

my appreciation of your loyal and devoted service

as a member of the Women's Land Army from

5th May. 1945.   to   26th October. 1950.

Your unsparing efforts at a time when the victory

of our cause depended on the utmost use of the

resources of our land have earned for you the

country's gratitude.

Elizabeth R

Chapter One

Early life in the Black Country

I was born in Old Hill, in the Black Country on the outskirts of Birmingham. It was an area which produced heavy industry and was renowned for chain-making; the large anchor for the Titanic was made there. In the past, there were many coal mines and when they closed, the slack, which is a form of compacted coal dust, was left in mounds. Eventually nature took over these and covered them with sparse grass. These areas were ideal playing places for children. Also at the back of the house there was an enormous marl hole where bricks were made. This gives an idea of the type of area where I was born and bred. My mother had a greengrocers' shop combined with a florist business, my two sisters worked there serving in the shop and making wreaths and wedding bouquets. It was a trade that required hard work. The shop was kept open very late at night, families were large and very closely-knit, and attitudes to funerals were different from today. Many more wreaths and flowers were sent from neighbours and money was collected.

Communities were closer and people helped each other, many were related as people did not move as they do now. Today's children are brought up to be wary of strangers and consequently are afraid to speak to anyone. So much has been lost in our society. Neighbours always had curtains drawn across as a mark of respect. Funerals were usually very early in mornings, so

The author, 5th May, 1943.

My mother's shop 'Walker's' at 206 Halesowen Road, Old Hill.

this required my mother and sisters to stay up most of the night to enable them to get the wreaths and flowers ready in time. Being the only florist, orders were taken from other shops in the surrounding districts, so this considerably increased the workload. During the day there was still the greengrocers shop to attend to, and at Christmas time it was a nightmare with wreaths of holly, artificial flowers and laurel being made. In addition to the usual busy trade, again people showed respect by placing wreaths on graves. The whole family helped during the busy time, so we were all used to hard work.

I was the youngest of eight, my brother Eric was three years older than me and after leaving school, was sent for one year to Clarkes Training College in Dudley. It was for a course in Typing, Shorthand and Book-keeping, and I was expected to do the same when I left school. I wasn't very good at studying and the thought of failure worried me very much, so I refused to go. I couldn't explain to my mother how I felt as she was very busy and didn't have time to listen to my problems. I loved animals, especially dogs, and I would take any of the neighbours' animals for walks.

Despite the industries, there were plenty of areas to play, the spoil banks had wild flowers growing on them and wild life thrived. One area had a particular attraction for me, this was situated at the back of a factory called British Casting. It was fascinating to watch the men pouring hot metal into the moulds. The factory backed onto a piece of land where the scraps of metal had been tipped to level the ground: it sloped off to a lower level and a small pool had formed. Here there were a range of pond creatures including many varieties of newts. We had a large aquarium at school so I always kept it well stocked. I had collected newts one day and they were all in a large jar in our back yard. However, the next day the jar was empty! I accused my mother of getting rid of them because she had complained – but she denied it. Months later they were found very much alive in large bags of sphagnum moss which were being piled high and were brought in for the Floristry Trade. Being amphibious, they had found ideal conditions.

Unfortunately, we didn't have a garden at home and this was something that I would have loved as I was always very interested in gardening. Instead the yard was bricked over to provide space for the business boxes and crates.

Chapter Two

Joining the Women's Land Army and going to Moulton Agricultural College

When I left school I got a job in the neighbouring suburb, Cradley Heath, at the shop next to Woolworths, called the Valeting Service. This was in 1940 during wartime, when women were called up and had to go into the services: WAFS, ATS, The WRENS and the Land Army or do factory work. Some work was exempt, if the work was important to war time it was known as a reserved occupation. Although I was only a shop assistant, my job did come under this category – however I wanted to join the Women's Land Army and even went to join at Broad Street in Birmingham when I was 16. I wasn't accepted because the entry age was 17 years. As my birthday was in October, I didn't want to start during the winter, so I waited until I was 17 and a half, and joined in May 1943.

In May 1943 the UK was facing serious food shortages due to the blockade of imports and the reduction in the workforce involved in agriculture in the UK. Food rationing was introduced on 8 January 1940. The weekly ration per person was butter 2oz, sugar 12oz and bacon or ham 4oz, per person per week. To buy most rationed items, each person had to register at chosen shops and was given a ration book with coupons in it. The shop keeper was provided with enough food for registered customers.

Other reductions in rations followed:

Food	Per person per week	Derationed
Butter	2 oz	May 1954
Sugar	8oz	September 1953
Cheese	1oz	May 1954
Tea	2oz	4 October 1952
Eggs	1 per person	26 March 1953
Sweets & chocolate	2oz	February 1953
Meat	1 shillings worth	4 July 1954

Continual rain ruined Britain's wheat crop so bread was rationed from summer 1946 until 1948. The long hard frost in the winter of 1946–47 destroyed most of the stored potatoes, and potato rationing was introduced. I decided I wanted to be part of the WLA and help to improve the food supply in this country at a very difficult time, after the end of the war.

I felt very excited when I was sent for, and also a bit apprehensive as I had never been away from home before. However I had notification to travel to Moulton Agricultural College in Northampton. There I commenced my training and I didn't realise then how fortunate I was to get training, I later discovered that many Land Girls were "just thrown in at the deep end" so to speak. When I reported to College I was shown my room, yes, we had a room to ourselves! Then we had to return downstairs to collect our uniforms.

After wearing ordinary civilian clothing, the uniform looked monstrous, it consisted of: 2 pairs of breeches; 1 green jersey; 3 brown aertex shirts; brown overcoat; 2 pairs of dungarees; gumboots; hobnail boots; sou'wester oilskin coat; 1 hat; 6 pairs of long stockings; shoes; 2 milking coats and a badge.

We had an armband which was green with a red Royal Crown on it and was worn above the left elbow; good service badges in the form of red half diamonds outlined in green were awarded after six months satisfactory service. Another was added within the next six months. These half diamonds were sewn onto an armband, then a two year special armband was awarded and these continued in different colours as satisfactory service continued. My final armband was yellow edged in green with additional diamonds to represent seven and a half years. Special ties were available and an extra charge was made for these.

On the next day it was raining and we had to put on oilskins which were stiff and we couldn't bend our arms, in addition to other heavy clothes and boots. We may have thought the clothes were heavy and rough looking but we soon discovered how necessary this was when we started the training. The first week was exceptionally tough, we were using muscles we had never used before and for at least a week I ached all over – not knowing whether it was easier to sit down or stand up. We were put on jobs for three days at a time, feeding and mucking out pigs, poultry; milking by hand and machine; learning to harness and drive a horse and cart and field work.

Evenings were spent in a Dutch Barn sitting on bales of straw listening to lectures. I was naïve because I was amazed to learn that a cow had to produce a calf before she gave milk! Some of the girls at the College were daughters of farmers so they were not as ignorant about farming as I was.

I particularly remember, when working with poultry, that they were housed in ark-shaped pens, no battery hens there. After being out all day we had to get them inside. The stupid birds had us running around everywhere

A postcard from Moulton. Moulton Agricultural College, where the author spent five weeks training, is in the top left corner.

before they would go into the pens and it was well after 11 o'clock before we retired. It was my last day on poultry and the next day was my first day milking, I can't remember exactly what time but milking was always a very early start. So between the poultry and milking, I had very little sleep.

We didn't get a lot of free time but I do remember several of us going by bus to Northampton. It was quite a novelty to get dressed up in our walking-out uniform. I had great difficulty keeping my hat on and somebody lent me a very large needle, we could get very little in those days. Northampton was crammed with various service men and we certainly attracted a lot of attention. I remember an American soldier following us everywhere, also a Scottish airman was saying something I failed to understand until I finally realised that he was referring to my substituted hat pin. After the first day out in the new uniform we returned to Moulton Agricultural College.

I had always been interested in the countryside and had a great affection for animals, so although my knowledge of farming was completely nil, I adapted very quickly. Milking cows held no fears for me at all as it did for many of the girls. If a cow was fidgety and inclined to kick, I was eager to show off my skill at handling the job and I would volunteer to take over. Our training should have been for four weeks but I was kept on for one more week to help the staff in readiness for the next group of land girls to arrive. I think it was because of my confidence and eagerness that I was selected to stay on. At last I was doing a job that I thoroughly enjoyed, no inferiority complex anymore. I vaguely remember some agricultural show being held there and some titled person visiting.

When we first arrived at Moulton, we were weighed and told that thin girls would gain but fatter ones would lose weight. After our four weeks, this proved to be correct and I certainly found muscles I never thought I had before.

The author's final WLA armband.

Chapter Three

Starting work at Barby Road, Rugby

So the time had come to start thinking of the next job and where it would be in Warwickshire. We each received notification and I was to go to Barby Road, Rugby. This road consisted of large houses owned by wealthy people surrounded by acres of land. The job seemed more like the 'Good Life' combined with a modest version of 'Upstairs, Downstairs'. There were two Jersey cows, poultry, ducks, geese, rabbits and a large garden where another Land Girl was employed. She lived locally at home. After my wonderful training and hoping to work with a pedigree herd of cows, I was very disappointed. I was offered a room in the house or I could use the harness room which was set up as a bedsit, situated next to the garages.

The harness room was very full of various harnesses of every description. The garages contained several large, expensive cars that were no longer in use because of wartime shortages. I was quite excited about using the room and thought I would be more independent there. There were two pigs housed not far away! The house was very large and in the past it had employed many people. They still retained a person who had been a personal maid but now had to extend her duties and there were several other staff including cleaners from outside. I had my meals with the other staff in a large room adjoining the kitchen. A cook from the next property came part time to prepare and part-cook the food. She worked at another large property in the Barby Road which belonged to an American. She was the only person there and it had no livestock but had previously stabled a string of polo ponies. They had all been destroyed owing to a shortage of food.

It was an exceptionally large house with accommodation for many servants. On the top floor there were many bedrooms lining each side of the corridor, all empty now of course. The part-time cook was named Hildegarde and she was Austrian. She had to report to the police periodically and she was not allowed to go out after dark. We became great friends. There were two riding horses on our property and she was a keen rider so we frequently went riding together. I couldn't ride, but I soon learned. One horse was a beautiful and well-disciplined hunter and the other was smaller and less manageable. Guess which one I rode, the smaller one! I think it must have belonged to a milkman, because every side road we approached it tried to turn into it. Persuading it to go otherwise caused it to slide and slither about. Trying to catch the horse was also a game of wits. The hunter would be approachable and no problems, without it I doubt we would have caught the other one because wanting to stay close was the only way of grabbing the top of its mane. We had to be wary of it whizzing around and kicking before catching it, it would have galloped around the field bucking like a mad thing.

Living in the Black Country my only contact with horses was seeing them pulling carts in the street. The local man selling ice-cream was an Italian named Verracho, who used to stop at my mother's florist shop for a flower of his choice which I remember was placed in a silver holder on his lapel. I used to feed his horse with a carrot.

The family seemed, to me then, very mixed up, as both husband and wife had families from previous marriages and now had a family together (it wouldn't be out of place nowadays). George was the son from the husband's previous marriage and came to stay. He was studying at Cambridge. I couldn't move anywhere without him and he followed me around like a little dog. His step mother told me to tell him to go away if he bothered me. Most weekends I had to work, having one weekend off in three. The weekend I was going home to Birmingham, George decided to come with me. I remember being very embarrassed on the train by George's very loud, cultured voice, aware that people were listening. He stayed at the Station Hotel in Birmingham. This was a very upmarket place where many uniformed officers were staying. I was invited to lunch there and was in awe at the splendour of the place and at the same time highly nervous as I had never encountered anything so top class. I wasn't sure what to order for lunch so George advised the partridge dish which had very small bones. I was really embarrassed trying to juggle them. I was sure everyone was watching. I had to invent a story to tell my mother that I'd been out with a girl friend.

One day I was asked if I could kill a chicken for the table. It had been explained when training how to go about it, so puffed up by my ego, I set about it. I did the job alright but thought it would be an instant death, it worried me that the wings were still fluttering and so this was the first and last I ever killed!

I had quite an embarrassing time one day when Mr B came into the dining area and said he would like to go riding with me and to saddle the horse. I didn't want to go and all the staff were twittering with indignation. His wife was pregnant at the time. What could I say? However, the horse saved the day, it had escaped from the field. Needless to say, I made no attempt to catch it!

There were many aspects of the job that I enjoyed including horse riding, my friendship with Hildegarde, plenty of good food and all the vegetables because all the produce went into the house. The milk from the Jersey cows was rich and made butter and cream. However, apart from my short time training I was not gaining experience with farming. After joining the WLA full of ideas and hopefully thinking my efforts would help in supplementing the food shortage I was despondent to find I was helping one household instead. I finally visited my representative explaining that I wanted to move and why. She was a friend of the family and was rather sarcastic about how I had enjoyed the horse riding. However, at the same time she couldn't argue with my reasons.

Chapter Four

Holt Farm, Studley, September 1943

I had a letter from Holt Farm, Studley, near Redditch. The farmhouse was situated on the main road with large farm buildings at the side. Contained within were stables, yards and small pens to house various animals. The milking area where we milked about 25 cows was also within the building. There was a farmer, his wife and one son, plus two men employed. Another girl was also employed and we worked together. A large pen housed the bull. At the back of the building was a Dutch Barn, which had bales of straw for bedding and various cattle food, all very convenient.

When working on a private farm we had an area representative to help with any problems that may arise. The work she did was invaluable. The farmer's wife had refused to accommodate us although the farm was quite adequate in size. The representative was not pleased because milking was a dirty job with unsociable hours, working with animals and coping with the milk and muck, especially when they are wet after being in the rain and mud. So, finding accommodation was very difficult. I had three different billets altogether, to be described later!

We started work at 7a.m. The cows were brought in and chained up in a stall. There was a rack for hay and a trough for food. Each cow had the same place and knew exactly where to go. First the udder was washed, then each teat was tested to make sure the milk was not infected, mostly by mastitis.

After milking each cow, the milk was put into large buckets and carried out of the building to the dairy which was at the back of the house. Here we needed strong arms to lift the buckets up and pour it into a container where it trickled over a metal ridged appliance with water running through it to cool the milk, before filling a churn which was placed underneath. One day my colleague didn't quite make it and the milk spilled over her. Eventually the churns were rolled out ready to be collected. The cows were let out and we returned to our billets for breakfast.

All the dairy utensils had to be scrupulously clean and put into a large chest to be sterilized. This was very hard on the hands, especially in cold weather. Then back to the cow shed to do the mucking out and washing down, hay put into the racks and food into the troughs. All ready now for the next milking. This routine had to be carried out every day. So weekends were limited to one off in every three including Bank Holidays. Our holiday entitlement was one week annually!

There were many other jobs around the farm in addition to milking.

Lifting mangolds was a particularly hard job. They were a large swede-like vegetable which were difficult to get out of the ground in cold weather, and with large leaves they were very wet but provided food for the cows in winter. Many other jobs had to be done including hoeing weeds, feeding pigs, helping with sheep and potato picking. Haymaking and harvesting also meant working overtime and was particularly hard work without the mechanical technology used today. A machine cut and tied sheaves and we had to stook them, which meant standing them up and putting eight sheaves together to enable them to dry. When it rained, they had to be moved around and given a good shake, by this time they were quite heavy. Every advantage was taken to get the cereal cut, dried and stored in a rick. Double summer-time was introduced for that purpose. The farmer told us we would be working overtime and I remember one evening it was 10.30p.m. when I finally returned to the billets. Food and drinks were supplied to keep us going. So before my eighteenth birthday I was starting work very early and finishing extremely late. Eventually when dry enough the sheaves were collected and made into a rick, and thatched to stay over winter until a threshing machine was brought in to separate the cereal. This was an exceptionally dirty and dangerous job. No health and safety rules then! As the rick was opened up mice and rats emerged and ran out having lived in the rick over the winter. It wasn't pleasant but we had to accept it. Nests of their young were found naked and blind. Wire netting was usually put around the rick to prevent them escaping, with dogs there to finish them off. When recalling these events to friends their reaction is one of horror. We had to accept the reality!

I also had the job of feeding 30 small pigs which were housed in one of the indoor yards. At first, whilst they were small, they were easy to feed and the food was distributed into 4 troughs. However as they grew bigger they would charge at me and the food was spilled. The solution was to put raw potatoes outside, then let them out and shut the doors. That gave me time to distribute the food easily, later letting them back in again. That worked well until as they grew, they scoffed the potatoes quicker and when I opened the doors to let them back in, they had vanished. They had gone quite some distance down the fields so I had to bang on a bucket with a stick and shout "Pig! Pig!". They came charging back with great speed. It greatly amused the passengers in a bus passing by.

The poultry used to wander in and out of the Dutch Barns and also in the rack where the hay was for the cows, to lay their eggs. Consequently, many were broken, so I saved as many as I could. When I asked if I could buy some to give to the housewife where I was billeted – the answer was no! I could easily have stolen them but I didn't, however, I collected no more.

My hopes of working with a pedigree herd of cows were again dashed because this farmer was a dealer and continually bought and sold livestock. There was no getting used to cows because they were constantly changed. Some of the cows were difficult after the trauma of being shunted around markets. One of the cows especially so, I milked her in the evening after she arrived and she was quite placid but my colleague couldn't get near her with the milking machine next morning. So, feeling confident, I said I would do it.

Before getting the final teat in place all hell broke loose. The machine was bashed apart and I was badly kicked, ending up in the gutter and hitting my face. I was very shaken and went over to the dairy to get cleaned up. There, to my disgust, I was given a cold cup of tea, nowhere to sit down and not a word of comfort. I was so angry I went back to work and probably recovered quicker by doing so! It was discovered later that the cow was blind in one eye and we had milked her on the blind side. How sad and confusing for the poor animal. Another time in the winter months when the cows were kept in at night chained in their stall, a calf had been born overnight. It was quite cold as the cow had been unable to lick any warmth into it. I vigorously massaged it and then carried it into one of the small pens, then released the cow and put them together. It could have been her first calf, because it seemed as if she was going to attack it. Eventually she settled down. She was a white cow with very long, upright horns. Next day one of the men went in to clean her pen out and she refused to let him in, so she had become very protective of her calf. I had no problem entering.

Cows and cattle would constantly arrive and depart. About 12–15 yearlings (young cattle) came in one day with stick-on labels from the market. These were quickly removed and next day they were sent to another market.

Whatever the short-comings, they were compensated by the satisfaction of being in a job I loved, being with animals and in the countryside observing nature. Some winter mornings in the building, a beautiful barn owl would be silently flying around – a wonderful sight.

I was also very fortunate because I had a good social life, some girls had a very tough time and were very isolated. There were many farms here in close proximity where other girls worked and also in a hostel in nearby Alcester. Our representative was a very good organiser and brought us all together. I also met a farmer's daughter from Lower Spernal Farm. We immediately became friends and remained so until she died. I was invited to the farm to meet her family. I was enchanted by the place, it was like looking at a beautiful painting (see page 25). The out buildings were half-timbered with a cow shed within a circular yard. There was a pond with ducks and geese. The farmhouse was very large and impressive. It had been part of the Estate of Coughton Court, until a member of the family gambled the money away, then it was taken over by Crown Properties. Her parents were very welcoming and it was like a second home for me. I spent many happy hours there. From the front garden of the house and across a field the river Arrow flowed. The area was rich with wild life. The bird life was fantastic and the nightingale could be heard singing in the stillness of a warm evening. At the back of the house overlooking the cowsheds, swallows were a joy to watch flitting around the yard and skimming the pond for insects to feed the young in their nests, many had nested in the cowshed.

The farm had two dogs, a collie and a small brown spaniel which was never chained and was very friendly. He would gently take a garment, coat or skirt, in his mouth and proceed to lead the person into the house. One day three of us, Joan, Joan's mother and I went on a duck 'safari'. Apparently their domestic ducks used to mate with wild ones down the river, so we went to collect the ducklings. Armed with large baskets and wearing wellingtons we proceeded along the shallow part of the river. The ducklings were very agile and would dive down as we tried to grab them. Eventually we caught quite a few along with their mothers. One unusual sight was to see two goslings following a hen. Joan used to put goose eggs under the hen to be hatched and they regarded her as their mother in spite of their difference.

The sheep on the farm always gave birth to lambs as early as January, so consequently they needed extra care. Our weather was more predictable in those days and winters were much colder. Joan took a weakling and nursed it by feeding it through the night and keeping it warm with hot water bottles. It grew very tame, very large and probably didn't regard itself as a sheep because it wouldn't go near the flock.

Joan had a collar and lead and we used to take it for walks, mostly along by the river, a walk I never got tired of. So peaceful with willow trees gnarled with age bordering it and passing by hedges and meadows. The grazing animals were surrounded by nature, with Coughton Court in view. In part of the river there was a place suitable for swimming which the family used and called it the "swimming hole".

In the winter nights Mrs Palmer, Joan and myself used to sit in the small cosy room near the Kitchen warmed by a lovely log fire. There was no

Lower Spernal Farm with Hereford Cattle where Joan was located, close to Studley.

electricity so we had paraffin lamps. We would be knitting and happily chatting. We had no TV or the present technology which in my opinion prevents conversation! I think it could be the cause of loneliness, especially for older people. I am now deaf which makes it difficult even to hear the conversations. Sadly missed!

Going home in the dark nights was always an ordeal because I had to go up a steep hill and although I tried to ride my bike to the top of the hill it was impossible and I had to walk. There were no lights in those days because of the war. One night I suddenly encountered a loud noise in the hedge beside me and I nearly jumped out of my skin. I think it was a horse. I also used to take Joan to my home and my family were very fond of her. My mother used to get our large family together about once a month, in the winter we were at home and in the summer months we had picnics in a nearby country area. My brothers used to organize games and we had some fun together. Joan really enjoyed herself.

The Land Army granted us only one week for our annual holiday. We decided to go to Bournemouth and booked into a YWCA hostel. We travelled by train the evening before and stayed in the waiting room to gain an extra day. I remember sitting there feeling very uncomfortable, with a shady looking character opposite us. Then a uniformed station employee came in and in a very stern voice he asked us what we were doing there. We felt guilty as if we had committed a crime. He left briefly and then reappeared. "Come with me" he said and we nervously followed crossing over the railway track to the opposite platform, not knowing what was going to happen. However, surprise, surprise, he unlocked a 1st class waiting room and said, "I am going to leave you here and lock you in until the morning". At last he smiled and said "have a comfortable night's sleep". It was luxurious with two very comfortable sofas and a well-equipped cloakroom. Luxury indeed! We were let out next morning and expressed our thanks for such comfortable accommodation. We couldn't book into our rooms until 12 noon so we were able to look around. We enjoyed our week and went to several afternoon tea dances. One soldier I danced with many times was having great difficulty getting acquainted with his young

On holiday in Bournemouth.

The author's friend Joan Palmer.

son. It was their first meeting and the boy screamed whenever he went near, just one of the sad things that happened in wartime.

We met a charming airman the first day and he accompanied both of us for the rest of the week. We exchanged addresses and photographs and corresponded. Unfortunately he was moved back to Canada shortly after we met and we didn't see each other again. It really was a love match and he hoped I would go to Canada. He sent photographs of his home and the surrounding area including a photograph of a miner working in a gold mine – that was his job. My mother was very upset and persuaded me not to go after putting every obstacle she could think of in the way. So, that was the end. I still have the photographs and wonder if he still has mine. I doubt it!

My social life continued to be enjoyable with the company of Joan and her family, the WLA club and its activities and the beautiful countryside with an abundance of wildlife. However, I continued to have problems with billets. It was not easy for the representative to find me a suitable place because of the nature of the job. The first place was an obvious mistake from the start, with a very nice family but a housewife who could not cope even before I arrived. The husband realised it shouldn't have been taken on in the first place and suggested I discuss it with the representative.

So another place was found, this place the opposite to the first with a very capable housewife with a very clean and tidy house. They had one daughter and another factory worker billeted there. I had to leave early to start milking at 7a.m., I usually made myself a cup of tea before going and then went back for breakfast. Milk and muck are not the most pleasant of smells and although I was used to it, it must have been very distasteful in the confines of a small house. I used to feel very uncomfortable at breakfast, in fact most of the time. The washing facilities consisted of a jug and a bowl in the bedroom, quite inadequate for my needs. There was a small separate building near the back door, used for washing clothes. It was very convenient for me to tidy up before entering the house, there I could get rid of hay seeds etc. I remember once after helping with the sheep, seeing a sheep tick crawling on my knee. Thank goodness I was able to destroy it before anyone saw it. It was unfair to the housewife as I also had to work weekends, having only one off in three. The factory worker, although employed on war work, had a very clean and tidy job and not unsociable hours like mine. She came home as clean and tidy as she left and earned far more money, also it didn't include weekend work. Remembering the late nights up to 11 o'clock in the evening when haymaking and harvesting were taking place, coming home exhausted and scratched with hair and clothing full of various seeds. Where girls were living in hostels the rules were strictly enforced to be in by 10p.m. However, I am not sure how this ruling would apply to living in billets or on a farm?

I sometimes went to stay overnight at Joan's farm for a week when her mother went away, to keep her company. It was an easy journey to the farm in the morning then I would go back to my billet for breakfast as usual, returning to Joan's later. Needless to say, they were delighted at my billets to give their consent for me to go! What a relief to use a bathroom with an inside toilet and the acceptance of farm and natural smells. Joan also milked the cows but it had to be done by hand because there was no electricity. We would go out to the poultry sheds to collect eggs, no battery hens there. The money from the eggs was usually a perk for the farmer's wife. Joan's mother was a wonderful cook and I still remember the taste of delicious home-made bread, butter and strawberry jam.

However, it was obvious that I would either have to move to another farm or find other billets. I talked it over with the representative who was well acquainted with Joan's family and with my reluctance to sever our companionship. We decided to give it another try to stay in the area. I didn't blame the housewife, she worked hard and did her very best but the conditions were just unsuitable for my tough physical job and with my difficult hours. Finally I was billeted with a family with two children, a boy of about 7 years and a girl around 9 years old, and the husband worked on a farm. In fact it was a fairly modern house allotted only to agricultural workers. My room had to be downstairs which seemed to be acceptable and luxury indeed with a bathroom and toilet. So life became less of a strain and problem solved.

Eventually, however, the unthinkable happened and this time it was a very different problem. The husband enjoyed a drink and one night he was out with an RAF friend, after a few drinks too many, the friend decided to invade my downstairs room which had no lock on it. The husband followed to remove him. I didn't make a fuss because no harm was done but I made sure that an item of furniture was put at the back of the door every night. So life settled down with improved facilities and I was contented.

Unfortunately it all came to an abrupt end. Coming back one evening from Joan's I had cycled to the top of the hill where it adjoined the main road and met the husband on his cycle coming home from the pub. Quite naturally we continued to cycle the rest of the way together. His wife was in the house next door with her neighbour and returned and accused us of being out together for the evening. I was furious and said I could prove where I had spent the evening. I made the decision that I had to move to another farm. I told the wife to ring Joan's farm for confirmation. However, that meant in those days going to a phone box.

Communication wasn't easy then. I was very distressed to be accused of such a thing and contacted my mother and the representative immediately. Next day my sister came with the car to collect me and take me home. Fortunately, because we had a business we had use of a vehicle. The representative arranged for me to work at Lodge Farm, Alcester Heath and live in.

Chapter Five

Lodge Farm, Alcester 1944

It was near enough for me to visit Joan's farm but not as often especially at night with no lights. Two other Land Army girls lived in and I settled in with no worries and being based on the farm meant no travelling. We had no electricity so it was hand milking and drinking water had to be obtained from the pump. We had oil lamps for lighting and oil for cooking with an additional Primus stove.

The farm was part of the Ragley Hall estate belonging to the Marquis of Hertford. Mr Heard was a tenant farmer with his wife and son, John aged approximately 14 years old. It was a large house with two staircases. Obviously in past days many servants were employed. Part of the downstairs was let to a couple with a young girl. There was a large Kitchen garden at the back surrounded by a brick wall. Within the garden was a toilet with a very deep ditch beneath. The amusing part was that it had three seats, two slightly different sizes and the third for a child.

We had our meals in the large comfortable kitchen. One part of the kitchen had been altered from a very large fireplace, and I would imagine it had a wall oven for roasting meat. However, a much smaller fireplace had been built leaving a comfortable area where Mr Heard sat with his dog. Many cockroaches appeared from the back of the fireplace at night and scurried around. Nobody seemed very worried, how different from my previous billets. I recall that as a tenant farmer, Mr Heard received an invitation for us to go to a celebration at Ragley Hall attended by the Marquis. At that time it was being used as a hospital for servicemen, they were dressed in blue and known as "The Blue Boys".

The three of us shared a very large bedroom. Judy and Doreen shared a double bed and I had a single. The beds had very deep feather mattresses and were very cosy and warm. No central heating then and our large room could become quite cold. We had to start milking at seven and to make sure we were on time Mr Heard brought us a cup of tea – luxury indeed. We could hear his footsteps long before he arrived. There were about 22 cows to hand milk and no long walk to the dairy this time. I had very strong hands and quite liked hand-milking. How pleasant to go to breakfast together. The other two girls were older than me and generally went around together. I was near enough to Joan to continue riding my bicycle over there in the lighter nights and we also used to meet at the club in Alcester.

Our representative had decided to form a concert party and found some great talent. The programme was made up of singing, dancing and sketches. The first performance was 4th November 1944 at YWCA Broad

Opening chorus including Joan Palmer.

Warwickshire Women's Land Army

Alcester W.L.A. Signature Song

WE'RE the land girls of Great Britain,
The land of the strong and the free,
We keep the home lands fertile
In the name of liberty.
We'll milk, we'll plough, we'll reap and sow,
We'll feed the pigs and use a hoe ;
In all work on the land,
Oh, we will take a hand,
We'll strive and strain with might and main
Till the men come home again.

We're the land girls of Great Britain,
The land in which we dwell,
With its hills and vales and downlands
And its pastures rich as well.
In the open air we can never shirk,
For we're healthy, strong and gay,
And here we mean to stay
And do our part with a willing heart
Till the men come home again.

Y.W.C.A., BROAD ST., BIRMINGHAM
SATURDAY, NOV. 4th, 1944, at 4-30 p.m.

The Alcester W.L.A. Club
PRESENT :

A · REVUE

—— *Arranged and Organised by* ——
Mrs. ADKINS & Mrs. HOLLAND

Compere : M. ADKINS
Accompanists :
Mrs. T. ADAMS and NORMAN STEED
Stage Manager : TERRY ADAMS

*In Aid of the Warwickshire Women's
Land Army Benevolent Fund*

PROGRAMME SIXPENCE

PROGRAMME

Artistes :

E. Ashford	E. Curtis	C. Hook	E. Perry	E. Rachael	M. Swift
V. Bishton	W. Cooper	L. Kendall	J. Palmer	O. Rubery	P. Thomas
P. Champkin	J. Danks	F. Mason	L. Player	E. Rushbrook	I. Ward
P. Colfield	V. Haye	E. Morris	L. Quiney	B. Strain	

1 The Land Girls say : "Hello, Everybody"

2 "Here's to the W.L.A."

    F. Mason   L. Kendall   E. Morris
    I. Ward   V. Bishton   E. Perry

3 Sketch, "Matinee" ... O. Langford & P. Champkin

4 Sextette, "The Barcarolle" and "A May Morning"

    J. Danks   I. Ward   F. Mason
    E. Perry   V. Bishton   E. Morris

5 Pianoforte Solo, "The China Doll" ... E. Perry

6 Monologue, "Madame Joujou & Alphonse" L. Player

7 "Spinsters Three" V. Bishton, P. Thomas & F. Mason

8 "Cherry Ripe"
   "On Wings of Song" } ... ... Lilla Quiney

9 Sketch, "The Lost Property Office"
    E. Rachael and P. Champkin

10 "Isn't this a lovely day" ... ... F. Mason

11 Ivy Ward and her Mandoline

12 "Wilhelmina" ... ...Soloist, L. Kendall
    Chorus :
  P. Champkin O. Rubery E. Rachael E. Curtis
  E. Morris E. Rushbrook E. Ashford T. Hook

13 Sextette, "Rolling down to Rio" & "Moonlight & Roses"
    J. Danks   I. Ward   F. Mason
    E. Perry   V. Bishton   F. Morris

14 "Alexandra's Ragtime Band" ... ... V. Haye

15 "Interviews at Mike" ...
   Announcer : P. Champkin
   Evacuee : W. Cooper
   Land Girl : V. Bishton
   Farmer : L. Player

16 Song and Dance, "Sitting on a cloud" ... L. Kendall

17 "Oh, what a life for a 'Lidy' "
    E. Mason, V. Bishton and E. Morris

18 "The Last Rose of Summer"
   "Impatience" } ... ...L. Quiney

19 Finale

Alcester W.L.A. Signature Song (*see over*)

GOD SAVE THE KING

Street, Birmingham. Afterwards it was presented at many local villages. The money raised was donated to our Benevolent Fund. I was too shy to take part but helped in any way I could. My friend Joan took part in the opening chorus. When they performed at Alcester Town Hall, I was asked to fill in a place in the opening chorus which was a song and dance routine, I couldn't let them down even though I was very reluctant. We wore a short white skirt and short top leaving a bare waist. Both top and skirt had two navy ¼ inch bands stitched around, so with a white flat beret and white pumps it gave quite a nautical look. I don't know how I survived the ordeal! I was very nervous. After the concert had finished the Hall was open to dancing. There were quite a number of American service men there and I recall one of them shouted over "Gee you have a great pair of legs!" That embarrassed me even more.

Although there were Italian prisoners of war working on various farms we were told that now we would be working with German prisoners. We were horrified at the thought. At thirteen, at the beginning of the war, indoctrinated by propaganda, I can't imagine what I expected. Two of them came on a regular basis joined occasionally by a third one. They were both named Rudolf, one very young and one much older. They helped during haymaking and harvest time. Each morning when they arrived, older Rudolf greeted us with "Good morning" whilst the younger one walked away.

I usually drove the tractor, a very old one that kept stopping and had to be cranked with a handle, quite a heavy job. Before I could get off the tractor the young one rushed over to start it. He always walked away swearing. During wartime farmers had to plough ground that had never been ploughed before and this one hill was quite tricky. I was driving the tractor whilst one German was picking the sheaves up and the other placed them onto the wagon. That morning I mentioned the lack of a morning greeting! So, I was driving at an angle and being fearful, when a heavy sheaf came tumbling down from the load on to my back. As I looked around a voice from above said "Good Morning", at last a smile! We later found out that he had to join up at an early age and had then been taken prisoner. His family had been killed in an air raid, the misery of war. A more congenial atmosphere existed afterwards. Mr Heard always provided a small breakfast for the regular prisoners, no more than two or three, in case their food was insufficient. The older Rudolf showed us family photographs including one where the bride wore black!

My life was much happier now as living on the farm was less stressful and Mr Heard was very appreciative of my skill of working with the cows, and in his eyes, I could do no wrong. Something that proved very useful when Judy miscalculated the width of the gateposts and knocked one down when driving the tractor at harvest time. We were both driving tractors with loaded trailers from the fields of wheat to the area where they were put into a rick, returning empty. One trailer had a faulty connection and was loose so it was out of alignment, going through the gate needed special care. Judy asked me to tell him, of course there was a string of expletives because it was a very busy time and it created extra work.

Mrs Heard was easy to get on with and we enjoyed each other's company. There were WLA rules, the main one to be in by 10pm at night. It applied to girls billeted in hostels and private billets. The hostels were very strict and many friends had stories to tell. Two of them were only 30 minutes late and the warden refused to let them in. The local police provided them with a cell for the night! Many managed to climb through windows or climb drain pipes helped by friends inside. However there were no restrictions at Lodge Farm. We didn't take advantage and it was great not to have to worry, and most of the time we were tired anyway with the hard work. However, the back door would be left unlocked for us.

One night I was invited to a special evening dress event quite a distance away. I told them I would be going and I wasn't worried about being late until I found the back door locked. My escort had a large torch and tried to help me find another way in. He had to leave and I kept the torch. I was reluctant to wake them but had no alternative. Mr Heard came down swearing, making me even more nervous. He unlocked the door to find himself in a searchlight beam and he scuttled away as fast as he could. I was worried and didn't know how I would face him the next day. However Mrs Heard thought it was quite hilarious because when her husband had come

This is the real image of a Land Girl! Not the dressed up on we see on TV. Lodge Farm, Alcester Heath, September 1945.

down he had a short nightshirt on and didn't want to be seen. He told her that as he opened the door he was dazzled by my light so he wanted to get out of sight as quickly as possible. On the way down, he hit his toe on the table leg, that made him swear! He was teased for some time afterwards.

Mrs Heard also organised a 'Ball' in aid of Cancer Campaign at the Town Hall in Alcester. Everyone wore evening dress. It was always exciting getting dressed up but quite difficult trying to see with only candles and oil lamps. Other dances we attended, we had to travel to by bicycle and so hoped it wouldn't rain.

Mr Heard and John used to ride with the local hunt during the season and we usually had lots of riders coming through. They also kept two young fox hounds until they were old enough to join the pack. We used to get visits from the WHIPPER-IN (the person dealing with the pack). I was fascinated listening to the stories. Another interesting group to visit were women with a pack of Beagles to hunt the hare. No horses, but followed on foot, very county types. Mrs Heard put on afternoon tea. She let me come and watch from upstairs where we had a very good view, we saw the hare running around in circles with the pack a short distance behind, following exactly. I can't remember if they ever caught anything!

There was one incident when the Heard's son John played truant from school, and I had to cycle round to find him. We didn't let him forget that!

My one week's holiday was spent in Bournemouth with my friend Joan following the same pattern, going the night before and staying at the YWCA as before. Again there were still many Canadian RAF there and we met them at the dances. This time I met a French-Canadian airman; I wasn't attracted this time as before. He wanted somewhere to spend his week's leave so we arranged for him to stay at an olde-worlde place near the farm. During the day he helped on the farm and had his meals with us. During war-time even if we had a camera, we couldn't get films, but he was able to take some photographs and they are still treasured today. One special one was when a group of us went on a trip to Stratford Theatre and our transport was an open lorry. We sat on the floor with no overhead covering, thank goodness it didn't rain! That was 22nd September 1945, the play 'The Merry Wives of

Windsor'. One photograph that I really treasure is of me dressed for work with the cows, dressed in dungarees, thick heavy shoes and a head scarf – really looking the part for my job of milking – unglamorous. Unlike the TV series, wrongly named 'Land Girls', I have been unable to watch it for very long because it is so inaccurate. Girls were working in pretty blouses and very clean smart dungarees, it gave no indication of the very arduous work we did! Some of the photographs of the concert party and trip to Stratford Theatre were printed in the Alcester Millennium Magazine.

Judy and Doreen decided to have an evening barbecue up in the woods nearby. They invited their RAF boyfriends and unbeknown to me a third one. Unfortunately, it happened when the Canadian friend was there and created embarrassment. However, it was fun lighting the fire and cooking the food that Mrs Heard had provided for us. Next day we almost fell asleep milking the cows.

The war was now over so Judy and Doreen decided to leave the WLA. I was quite sad to see them go. My friend Joan came over to stay on occasional weekends, there was now a big empty bed. I remember we were in bed and there was the sound of rats running around in the roof. Although a farmer's daughter, Joan was horrified! The rat population on the farm was increasing rapidly and Mr Heard wasn't getting anything done about it. At night, when I came in on my bike, the light would show up many pairs of eyes. I used to kick the shed door open and straighten my front wheel and throw the bike in! I may have encountered many rats while working on the threshing machine but that was enough! Mr Heard used to take the terrier out and get rid of a few.

To replace the two girls, two boys were employed. They were unused to farm work, one was a Londoner and the other Welsh.

It was always a very busy time when the pig was killed. I helped Mrs Heard in the kitchen, although it wasn't Land Army work to be working inside! So much to do, making sausages, chitterlings (pigs' intestines) and many other jobs. I remember Auntie Lilian, Mrs Heard's sister came to help – she was a favourite of mine, quite a character. She made wine and her speciality was – Rook Pie! Farmers used to shoot them because they were numerous and would reduce the crops.

At Christmas time, when the family were out visiting – they left the boys and myself with some refreshments and some of Aunt Lilian's wine. The boys tucked in and drank the wine, needless to say that it was very potent. Fortunately, I didn't drink much – I think it was parsnip!

Very often quite a few of Mrs Heard's family visited, they were also farmers and lived near Evesham. Mr Heard had a very broad Devon accent which I managed to understand most of the time, but the family didn't – so I found myself as an interpreter.

Part of my job was bottle-feeding the calves, a job I enjoyed even though they could be very frisky. The farm buildings were black and white half-timbered and the calves were housed in a small pen. I contracted ringworm which apparently lives in wood, so it probably came from there. It took some time to get rid of, it was scaley and blistery.

Another time Mrs Heard and the two boys went down with the flu, it was a problem to get the milk ready for collection. I had to fit in time to cook, something I didn't know much about, it wasn't an easy job with oil appliances! I had to work in the evening to prepare the food, then try to give some attention to the other jobs.

It was a nightmare and even though I was very tough, it was too much and I collapsed. The doctor was visiting the others and said I must rest. I did but not for very long.

There was a day when somebody walking through the farm left the gate open and the cows went into the adjoining field which was very large, it took a long time to finally get them in to milk them, fortunately it was in the afternoon so we didn't have to worry about collection. Many WLA had left by now but as the country was still short of food it continued until 1950.

The rats became a nuisance and could be heard moving about above the back door, where the ceiling was very low. I was terrified that they would come through into the house! The WLA were advertising for relief milkers with extra pay. Mr Heard was very old fashioned and didn't move with the times, he should have done something about the rats long ago. One day whilst milking, a rat appeared in the cow shed looking very dishevelled and just stayed there not moving. I decided I needed a change and applied for relief milking. For all my hard work Mr Heard had promised me a rise of 10 shillings but I think he forgot about it and I was too shy to remind him. They were very upset when I told them I had applied for another job. I was upset too but I really needed to move on. I enjoyed my time at the farm and after the experience of living in billets it was so much better. I still kept in touch and many years later I asked John about the rats. He said mange killed quite a lot of them.

Chapter Six

Gaydon Aerodrome

The next place was at Gaydon which was an aerodrome still occupied by a few RAF personnel. I quite enjoyed my short stay there. The Land Army occupied one of the RAF huts which I shared. It had beds on both sides and a stove in the middle – it was very comfortable and cosy. Being together is also very sociable, something that existed during wartime was sociability. People were very friendly and helped each other through the tough times. Something sadly lacking today!

The work here was different from private farming, they went to various farms doing different jobs when required. They either cycled or were transported by whatever transport was available. Though I was only there for a short time, I remember there was quite a disturbance when a large fire extinguisher, situated near the entrance was knocked over and suddenly produced a flow of white foam before it could be removed outside. What a mess!

I arrived there when I had my 21st birthday, but I didn't make it known to anyone. I finally met my new 'boss'. His name was Mr Perfect, unfortunately he had a terrible stutter which was quite embarrassing until I got used to it. I admired him very much when I heard that in spite of it he gave lectures. I spent about two weeks going to various places to see different milking machines, I didn't need training being knowledgeable about the milking routine. I started my first relief milking job at Barton.

Chapter Seven

Barton, near Leamington Spa

This time the farmhouse was modern and there was just the farmer and his wife. The cows were a pedigree herd of Ayrshires and the farmer was up to date with modern farming methods. Everything was going well, the farmer's wife was friendly and we got on very well together. The farmer suggested that the three of us should go to Leamington to a farmers' meeting, and that it would be of interest to me. However troubles unpredicted were ahead when it was suggested going to another meeting in Leamington. I naturally thought it included his wife, I was surprised when she said she hadn't been invited! I declined, I wouldn't have enjoyed it anyway.

This started an unbearable atmosphere between man and wife and was very embarrassing for me. This then opened up an explanation by the wife of a previous incident when two WLA were employed and without going into detail, caused her to attempt suicide! After that they were barred from employing WLA. This should have been checked before sending me. I hurriedly sent a message to Mr Perfect and he came immediately saying I was urgently needed to go to another farm. This is where living in a hostel was much better and no problems like this would occur. Also my weekends were now free!

Chapter Eight

Little Compton, near Shipston on Stour

So I went back to Southam hostel for a short time. On 28th November 1946 I started a job at Little Compton on a farm called King Stone Farm. It was a lovely old building and I was introduced to the farmer's wife in the large kitchen. She seemed quite a strong character, with cropped hair and smoking a cigarette. It was always difficult having to work and live in, not knowing what to expect. However she was a great character and we really hit it off. She showed me photographs of her younger days when she rode motorbikes and I really enjoyed her company. The cows were machine milked and I had the usual jobs.

One morning we set out on part of the farm on the top of a steep hill. It was a frosty morning and the view was marvellous. It was pointed out that four different counties could be seen. We were always being teased, so that when I was told that nearby there was a ring of stones, very ancient, and they leaned towards each other as if in conversation, and that they were called the 'Whispering Knights', I didn't believe any of it! I was told there was also another stone that was an 8ft tall part of the circle that was called the 'King Stone'. The Farm was named after it. The collective name was the 'Rollright Stones'. Of course, it was true.

On Sundays I joined the family going to Church and afterwards a group of young people came back to the farm and enjoyed a pleasant evening

The 'Whispering Knights'.

together. A group of us went carol singing, and that was good fun. Being a small village, people knew each other, not like today when next door neighbours are unknown to each other. We were invited into several homes and given a drink and food! For the first time I worked on Christmas Day. I almost felt part of the Christmas story, with the animals! It was a lovely place to spend Christmas Day and there was a large group of us. I remember the game 'Murder', in a large house with its two staircases, we were able to spread out. My time was also extended to allow me to attend the 21st birthday of a cousin. I finally sadly left but kept in touch with the farmer's wife and daughter for many years.

Chapter Nine

Grange Farm, Bidford on Avon

On 28th January 1947 I returned to Southam Hostel to prepare for my next job. What an experience was in store for me there! It was certainly unforgettable. I arrived at Bidford Grange Farm situated at Bidford on Avon near Stratford and not far away from Joan, my friend at Spernal. It was an old Manor House with nearby buildings which housed the various animals and the cowshed had about 15 cows milked by machine. The weather was atrocious and right from the beginning I started with a light covering of snow. The approach was about half a mile from the road. It was very different from Kingstone Farm and the atmosphere inside was as icy as the weather which was extremely cold. The farmer's wife once referred to me as a farm labourer! Well I laboured very hard under such harsh weather conditions, so I suppose it did apply. At the table one day she made a point of telling me, indignantly, that it wasn't right that farm labourers were allowed more cheese on their rations than farmers. This was whilst my apparent extra ration was being consumed by the family!

We didn't have TV or the convenience of mobile phones in those days and I was confined to the house because I was so isolated. Many years later I found details of the local history on a computer. It described various mills which existed there in the 15th century. However, the bad weather persisted until I left so I never even managed to see around the farm. I

Visiting Coughton Court with Joan Palmer, near to Bidford on Avon.

believe it could have been a manor house. I do remember the coldness of the bedrooms when the high winds were blowing and the windows rattled. It would have been possible to write my initials on in the frost on the inside of the window pane.

Milking was a very arduous job even when the weather was normal, but the continuous icy conditions created many problems. With the cows staying inside it meant extra cleaning and mucking out, then the feeding and of course the milking twice a day. With the strenuous work, I managed to keep warm, except when it came to milking. Then I had to use water to wash the udders which was disastrous for my hands. Any moisture on my hands when I picked up the metal milking machine almost ripped the skin off.

The ground was iced over every day and very hard, however in spite of that the farmer came along and said that the cows must be let out. I told him that was absurd and that made him even more determined! I reluctantly unchained them and let them out. Their legs were probably stiff after being confined, which didn't help when they came into contact with solid, frozen ground. They were slipping all over the place and in danger of breaking their legs. He realised his mistake and I was allowed to return them to the cowshed.

Although I can recall most of my experiences, some are forgotten and others are sometimes hazy. Luckily, I happened to find a note, whilst writing this, by my brother of his wedding day on 23 February 1947, a time when I was working at Grange Farm, Bidford. I had forgotten all about it! I had been puzzling about the weather and when it was at its worst, so now I knew that I obviously was able to travel home at that time. He described how hard times were, even worse than war time, how apparently potatoes and bread were rationed! He was disabled whilst serving in the army. He writes about how friends and neighbours sacrificed their meagre rations to enable them to have a Wedding cake made. They were unable to find a place to live and arranged to share a rented house with the bride's grandfather. He writes that it was either that or nowhere to live! Was this the repayment for fighting for our country! They had to buy furniture with coupons and there wasn't enough for a complete bedroom suite. Everything was rationed at that time, so back to the farm after the wedding. It must have been then that the weather became really bad and the blizzards piled the snow up high above the cowshed doors. I had the job of removing it to get into the cowshed.

The long drive was blocked, preventing anything from going in or out of the farm. It was eventually opened up by prisoners of war. The work on the farm became more difficult and I almost lost the use of the milking machine. The icy weather caused moisture to get into the tube that worked the pulsator and it had to be continually dried out. The farmer suggested putting it into hot water! I think NOT! Without the machine the cows would have to be hand-milked, that would have been difficult when they had always been machine-milked.

I had one weekend off in three and by now I was in need of a break. German prisoners had cleared the drive although there was still deep snow about. As it was my weekend off I was determined to get home. The farmer that I worked for at Alcester said I could stay there should I get stranded. So I decided to hitch-hike through the snow. I walked to the road and the first lift was a small coal lorry with a small cab and open at the back. The driver was a man with a beard, quite jolly. I got as far as Stratford. I was on the Alcester Road and there was deep snow piled on either side. I had several lifts as they got stuck in the snow, I just waited for another and by doing that I eventually reached High Street, Alcester. There was a bus! When I enquired about it I was told that it was now converted into a snow plough and was going to (hopefully) Birmingham. Passengers could travel at their own risk. So, we got through alright. How wonderful to be home!

Travelling back was easy now the roads were clear, there was still snow about though. Now the snow was beginning to thaw, it created another problem – flooding! The farm worker's cottage, by the river was flooded and they had to move upstairs. In the nearby village of Welford on Avon the river came above the bridge and a couple in their car turned off the main road and their car was submerged. The man survived but the woman was drowned, the body was found at Bidford. As if we hadn't had enough, we also had very strong winds and a very large tree was blown over at the front of the house. Fortunately it was away from the house and didn't do any damage. The snowiest British weather of the 20th century was in 1947, when it fell somewhere every day from January 22nd to March 17th. It was reported in the newspaper as the *"Worst Winter Ever – 1947"*.

Working in such conditions was very tough, especially when the farmer wasn't knowledgeable about the dairy side. It seemed that everything weather wise had happened: snow, ice, blizzards, high winds, floods and I did not have the most pleasant place to relax after working. I was therefore very disillusioned and now the war was over, land army regulations were relaxed to encourage us to stay because food shortages were more reduced than ever. I decided after my weekend off, I would just leave and not return. I was visiting my friends at Spernal, not far away, and Joan's mother advised me to go back and confront them with how uncomfortable life had been there, she said otherwise they would just get away with it! I stayed overnight at Spernal then cycled to Grange Farm early in the morning when the milking was about to begin. The farmer was surprised to see me. When I told him that I had decided not to return he said they had guessed that would be the case. However I explained the advice I was given, and I volunteered to help with the milking while I was there. He invited me to go to the kitchen for coffee and I knew his wife would be there. She said her husband had explained that she hadn't been very pleasant to me and if I stayed she would be pleasant. I said that if it wasn't natural it wouldn't be genuine! So that was final. The problem of working and living in the same place where it is necessary to confront a domestic situation can make things very uncomfortable.

Back to Southam Hostel April 1947 for instructions for the next job.

Chapter Ten

Fenny Compton Hostel and Grange Farm, near Banbury

Another surprise in store for me! This project was exceptional, designed to provide 4-5 farms with a relief milker for a day off each week, even on paper it seemed over ambitious. I don't think enough thought was put into it by whoever planned it. On some farms I was assisting another person and that worked very well, others expected me to walk in and take over alone.

It was impossible to estimate the changes that would occur within the dairy herd. Some were about to calve, some were in full milk and both of these were part of the daily routine. That was one problem, another was distance. I cycled to the farms, one was quite a distance away and the milking started at 6a.m. and I had to have a break for breakfast and lunch. I can't recall if breakfast was provided or not. Lunch would have been a packed lunch provided by the Hostel. It was such a long day and I needed to have a rest but had nowhere to relax. It was an unsolvable problem. I gave it a fair trial, but I suggested someone else should take it on, perhaps the person who set it up! The area I was working in was Fenny Compton, near Banbury and this was the first time I was living in a hostel.

As I was a relief milker it was still different work from the others who worked daily on various farms. Transport was provided for them or they used bicycles. Fortunately, one of the farmers from the last job needed help because the cowman had been kicked by a cow and had his leg broken in two places. The farm was a short walk from the hostel.

There were 30 cows to milk and I had to start work at 6a.m. This was a different set up and there was a milking parlour installed, something I hadn't encountered before. It was a much better idea than having all the cows chained up, carrying the milking machine from cow to cow and then carrying heavy buckets to the dairy. This was obviously the beginning of the present-day technology enabling cows to be milked in very large numbers.

When the cows were brought in they came into a large yard with two other smaller yards divided off. One of these was left open and led towards the milking parlour. The other was closed and they entered that yard when they had been milked and were leaving the unit. The milking parlour admitted four cows, there were two milking units, two cows were milked and whilst the machine was milking them the other two cows were prepared for milking. When milked the first two cows were let out into the other closed yard and two more cows were admitted and the milking continued until all were milked. The milk from each cow was automatically transferred to the dairy, no lifting or carrying of buckets of milk any more. Very time saving!

As they entered, each cow had food from a hopper (a container tapering downwards) released by the touch of a handle. The hoppers were filled up each evening from a room above, so that everything was ready for the morning milking. It was imperative to get everything prepared for the early collection of the milk.

It was a change to live in a hostel and I enjoyed the companionship. It was great getting back in the evening, going into the lounge and recounting the day's events. The others usually worked in small groups and their work was varied. I remember we played records and enthused over Frank Sinatra's music. The hostel was a wing of a large house and accommodated about twelve of us. Downstairs we had the lounge, dining room and kitchen. Upstairs there were three bedrooms and *one* bathroom. It was no use being modest, we all had to share. As everything was rationed in those day, the slogan was "the public should use water sparingly" i.e. they recommended five inches of water for a bath!

Grange Farm, Fenny Compton, 1947.

Some of our jobs required plenty of water afterwards especially when working on a threshing machine – the dust and dirt was horrendous. I wonder how we did it. However, as always during wartime we had to manage!

The bedrooms were inconvenient. I shared with another girl and our bedroom was also the entrance to the three bedrooms and one bathroom. This meant that everyone walked through it. Also our beds were placed either side of the doorway, leaving a way through which was only the width of the door. Everyone usually brushed past our beds as they passed. Steps led to the next two bedrooms and the bathroom. The third bedroom was approached through the second bedroom. There the beds were the double bunk type. I had to be up early enough to start milking at 6a.m. whereas the others started at 8a.m. With the arrangement of everybody coming through my bedroom it was difficult for me to get any extra sleep if I felt tired. I was very fortunate to share with someone who was reliable enough to make sure I was awake early in the morning.

So, to work in the morning; the cows were in a field nearby to enable me to start early. Incidentally, the bull accompanied the herd and was usually manageable. I did have a problem one morning with the mud. The weather had been very wet and in the mornings the cows tended to wait by the gate. I had to push it right back and I sank deep into the mud, it was quite a struggle to extricate myself! When the milking was finished and I had rolled the churns out for collection I had to light a fire in the boiler to provide steam to sterilize the dairy utensils which were placed in a large chest. Then I returned to the hostel for breakfast.

Returning to work, the cows had already been taken along a very narrow, gated road to a large field where they stayed until I brought them back for afternoon milking. In the meantime I had the usual routine jobs to do. Because of my early start, I had about two and a half hours allowed for lunchtime to adjust my hours. It was difficult to know how to spend the time. In the beginning, I decided to catch up on my sleep. Unfortunately this didn't work because I slept very heavily and was very drowsy and had difficulty when I went back to work. Consequently I never did that again. Instead I was able to rest and knit or darn socks, a job that needed doing constantly.

I had to ride a horse to get the cows back because the field was very large and a distance away along a gated lane. The horse was a very intelligent animal and knew exactly what was required. Sometimes a cow would continue grazing instead of keeping up with the herd. I would leave it, hoping it would run along and join us. However very often we would have to go back and then the horse would give it a nip and then push it as if reprimanding it. There was one occasion when the bull became very nasty and let the cows go on whilst he stopped and began pawing the ground, shaking his head and rolling his eyes. I wasn't sure what to do but I didn't feel safe on the horse. I got off and clapped my hands and shouted at him and gave him a hard slap on the backside. Luckily for me he went on and joined the cows, after all he was around all the time and was usually docile. There was only one other time I had trouble, that was when he came into the milking parlour and he was so big I had difficulty getting him out through the doors.

One morning I had quite a shock. I had forgotten to fill up the food hoppers for the cows which meant I had to go next door, through the stables where the horses were and up some very narrow winding stairs to a small room where I shovelled the food into the hoppers. It was very eerie there, but even more so when I heard footsteps coming up. I was very nervous and looked down the stairs to see the horse that I rode, climbing the stairs with great difficulty. It was even more difficult to push him down again backwards. All the time I was worried that I would be late with the milk. I didn't forget to put the food out ready again.

Periodically the milk was tested by, I think, the Milk Marketing Board for various things which included cleanliness. I am proud to say that I came somewhere near the top of the list twice for the area of Warwickshire. The farmer was paid more money and he was generous enough to give me a bonus!

The local soldiers' camp used to issue invitations to the hostel for their dances at the camp. An Army truck was provided for the journey. As we were isolated and transport limited, it was very much appreciated. It was there I met a Scottish soldier and we went out together for some time.

Now that the war had been over for three years, the Land Army was still needed because the food supply was even more desperate than before and didn't improve until the 1950s. However, many girls left and they even continued to recruit more. The small hostels were closed and the girls were moved into larger ones. This meant our hostel was closing – it was a sad time. I decided to move to Devon and give up the strenuous job of milking and have weekends free. Some of the cows I was milking were very restless and kicked. I remembered that I had taken over from the previous cowman, who had still not returned and had suffered from a kick that had broken his leg in two places. I also had bruised legs.

The farmer tried in vain to persuade me to stay, but I made my farewells and on 23rd April 1948, I arrived at Tenby House, Okehampton. This time the hostel was situated in town, so the social life was great. The house was bigger and although we had the usual double bunk beds, the bathrooms were better and not so public.

There were about six of us sharing a room. I soon became close friends with Joyce, a farmer's daughter from Axminster. She had been in the Wrens as a cook. We had several Wrens in the hostel, like many of us it was very difficult to adapt when leaving the service, so as the WLA still existed, they joined. It was great hearing about their experiences, especially June, a Londoner. Her life had been very interesting and I was enthralled listening to her although it was tinged with great sadness. Her fiancé had been a fighter pilot and was shot down, she received news of his death on her 21st birthday. Her family were all killed in the bombing of London.

While she was serving in the Wrens, she was fortunate enough to be chosen to go to Australia. About 10 of them went and she related some fascinating stories about their adventures. The ship they went over on was full of service men and they had to be protected from them! They were confined to areas within the ship and guarded. I can't recall what year it was or the reason for going, probably early in wartime and they had a tremendous reception from the Australians. I listened to the descriptions of Oz and saw lots of photographs. It must have left an impression on me because when I left WLA I went to Oz, as a £10 pom.

Chapter Eleven

Hostel at Okehampton, April 1948

Two of us transferred from Fenny Compton to Devon, unaware of what part of Devon we would be sent to, so Okehampton it turned out to be. It was situated to the North of the highest part of Dartmoor, very much a change from the flatness of Warwickshire. Travelling to work through narrow high-hedged roads, wild flowers grew in profusion and were a delight to see, even though great difficulty was encountered whenever another large vehicle approached and we had to drive backwards for what seemed to be long distances.

I remember one of our jobs was potato planting and some places were very, very steep and to stop them rolling we had to really push them into the ground. It was very tiring trying to stand up in those circumstances! Another job was to pick up stones from the ground which was littered with them, we never did find any buried treasure to relieve the boredom and backache. When the two of us arrived from Fenny Compton we were sent out the first time to a very small half-timbered cottage to a young farmer and his wife. They were a delightful couple and very friendly. We were invited in to eat our packed lunch and they provided us with tea. Unfortunately we were embarrassed because we had difficulty understanding the dialect, which I think was more pronounced in the rural areas and we hadn't had time to get used to it. I found myself nodding my head to avoid saying yes or no. Plants and some farm tools had different names. For instance, what we call bilberries, they called whortleberries.

There was a large white house on a hillside in the area that was a landmark for miles around and occasionally land girls were sent to work there. It was, if I recall correctly, owned by a wealthy bachelor who was looked after by a local couple, whom he regarded as family. Joyce and I worked there for a couple of days. We felt very privileged. The work was very easy and looking at photographs now, I see we were wearing our best uniform instead of the usual dungarees. We were asked what sort of cakes we liked and one was specially baked for us. We appreciated the kindness shown. Happy memories!

We used to go dancing on a Saturday and met two local lads studying at Cambridge. Peter asked if when he came some time would I like to go to the Cinema? I gave him my phone number to ring. In the meantime Joyce

Tenby House WLA Hostel, Okehampton, Devon.

Okehampton, Devon. The cups displayed here were won by the WLA whilst playing football against the local laundry girls.

constantly talked about the driver who took them to work and back. When we were out together one day, we met him and I was introduced. Then a very strange thing happened. I received a phone call asking if I would like to go to the Cinema; thinking it was Peter, I arranged to meet. The Cinema was just at the end of the road. Instead her "dream boy" turned up. Surprise, surprise, I even had chocolates. It was difficult to explain to Joyce but she understood. She finally met Fred and they eventually married.

Another event that took place was an annual football match between WLA and the laundry girls. I didn't play but cheered them on. Apparently the WLA always won, not surprising considering how fit we were with the tough work we endured.

I had a really enjoyable day when Fred took Joyce and me walking over Dartmoor to Yes Tor. It was swampy and dangerous but Fred was experienced. He carried a long stick to test the ground when necessary. I think it was about 4 miles from Okehampton but could be wrong. Yes Tor was regarded as the Giant of the Moor. There were many gruesome sights on the moor, where animals had been submerged in the swamp and then disgorged. The farmers had sheep there and I saw the sad case of a ewe and lamb that had died while lambing. I would imagine that it could be dangerous for any animals. The walk was very interesting and apart from the sad scenes, I thoroughly enjoyed it. We climbed to the top of the Tor with photographs to prove it.

Occasionally two of us used to go riding over the Moor. I don't consider myself a good rider and horses can usually weigh up the skill of a rider. We had great difficulty urging them away from home and were slow. However they certainly speeded up when homeward bound and we had a wonderful ride back.

We often heard of escapes from Dartmoor prison and one night when returning from a dance in a taxi we were stopped and searched by police. There were four of us all wearing evening dresses and there was a lot of fooling around suggesting he could be hiding under our dresses! For a late night like that we had to get special permission, otherwise the rules were that we had to be in by 10p.m.

Other incidents that happened included having to return home for a bunion operation. The first visit I made to hospital I caught a very bad cold so they were unable to operate, so I returned to Devon. My next visit was successful. Another time I had a blackout in the bathroom and hit my face on the corner of the bath. I went to work with a beautiful black eye and suffered the usual comments.

Chapter Twelve

Park Hall Hostel, Salford Priors

I really enjoyed my time in Okehampton, however with rumours going around that the hostel might close, I decided it would be better to return to Warwickshire where I would be nearer home. I applied for a transfer back and in April 1949 I went to Salford Priors, near Evesham.

The hostel was a very large building with about 26 rooms. In addition there was what was referred to as a cottage, but was in fact a fair-sized house also accommodated by WLA. There was a large wooden hut built on to the side of the house for recreational purposes. The house had been the former home of the late Lord Henry Seymour and Lady Helen Seymour. It was requisitioned by the BBC until 1943 when it was taken over by the WLA.

There were also other huts in the grounds and these were occupied by various people coming from the towns, such as office workers, who were given free board for a working holiday. We sometimes worked with them.

I remember potato picking, a job that was constantly bending down and very hard work. The potatoes had to be picked up quickly to keep up with the tractor. It was then that we usually helped them as we were used to the hard, physical work.

There were about sixty girls in the hostel. I don't know when recruiting stopped because the WLA was about to finish. However the difference in

Cabbage planting by machine at Bomfords in Dunnington, 1949.

age and experience was noticeable. The small hostel had closed and the girls were being transferred to larger hostels similar to this one. The area was mainly market gardening, growing strawberries, cabbages, beans and other vegetables. We went out either on bicycle or in a large lorry driven by a WLA girl. In the past many itinerants were employed in the high season to cope with the work. I did work with them once and they were hard workers and very interesting to talk to. Having travelled around they were very knowledgeable. They had been staying in the Bristol area and I remember them telling us about a large aeroplane being built – the Bristol Brabazon.

They sent me out relief milking to a farm not too far away in a small village called Broom. I knew of this farm because it had a pedigree herd of Ayrshire cows. The farm itself was very interesting, especially the barn. It was beautifully half-timbered and it was thought it may have been taken from a ship. I went there twice for two weeks each time, living in.

Most of us came from the Midlands and didn't stay in the hostel at weekends, but of course there were always some that did and some very strange things happened there. One incident we heard was a story about a man standing over a girl's bed with a large torch waking her, dazzling her and then moving away. As she sat up in bed her nightdress straps had been cut. In my opinion, as I thought she was what I might describe as frivolous, I didn't believe it. However he continued to invade the place and cut their clothes! He didn't attack but must have been very quiet and careful. I think they decided to be together in one room, it was a large building and would probably be easy to get in. We had a forewoman who was a very sensible person, she didn't usually stay weekends, but on this occasion she did and a very peculiar thing happened. She awoke to a loud scream from the room opposite where her friend was, as she put the bedclothes aside to get out of bed, she found her pyjama leg was flopping about. Her friend was dazzled by the torch and her nightdress straps were cut. I don't think anyone ever saw him or that he was ever caught by the police.

Getting home for weekends, we usually had to rely on lifts as buses were very infrequent. Transport was very varied. Once a new car carrier stopped

Relief Milking at Broom Court, Bidford on Avon, 1949.

piled high and invited us to climb right to the top. There were three of us and we managed to get to the top and stay on. We passed the double-decker bus where some of our friends were sitting on top deck and we were all laughing and waving. The embarrassing part was climbing down in Birmingham in view of everybody.

Another time about six of us were waiting and I wasn't in uniform because I was meeting a friend and I was planning to catch the bus. Then a motorbike stopped and I was pushed forward to go on it. I was trying to make gestures to indicate I wasn't suitably dressed and went to apologise but in vain. I was offered suitable gear to cover my coat, in fact top to bottom. It was quite embarrassing stepping into it and getting zipped up. The others thought it was really funny and fell about laughing. However, I had the last laugh when I saw them in town and they were dusty and dirty from whatever transport they managed to get!

The usual invitations were made to attend dances at Long Marston barracks or RAF camp and we would be picked up in transport provided, as we had no other means of transport. I didn't always go but occupied my time in other ways – making apple pie beds, with another friend, to give them a nice surprise when they returned. It meant folding the sheets so they couldn't get into bed. That caused a bit of a stir. When that became monotonous I accidently found something much better. The beds had folding legs! BRILLIANT, so two of us set to work and positioned legs so that the slightest weight would fold them in and collapse the end of the bed. Not forgetting I shared the room and had to pretend to be asleep and innocent! They had no doubt I was the culprit! It wasn't just my bedroom but others around it so it caused quite an upheaval. What also happened was some of the beds didn't go down until perhaps a week later. They were determined to get me by doing the same to my bed but I made sure I checked it before getting in. So my friend from London, Dot Adams, waited for me and decided to push me onto the bed. She pushed me backwards so my feet went upwards whilst she was facing the bed with her feet underneath where the bed was about to fall, it fell on her big toe which was bruised and black for weeks! That prank was not repeated, not only for the injury, but it was too noisy.

Now that I was near my friend Joan again it meant that we could meet and socialise together again. One event that we attended was at Studley where Joe Loss and his Broadcasting Orchestra visited on 18th November 1949. The tickets cost one guinea each. I still have my ticket put away in my WLA album with signatures of Joe Loss and about four members of the Orchestra. I wore a black lace evening dress. My mother sent a corsage for each of us – orchids, flowers that were very popular at that time. Our hostel had a beautiful staircase which was screened off to prevent anyone from

ENTACO RECREATION CLUB.

Second *Annual* *Ball*

at the

ENTACO HALL, STUDLEY,

FRIDAY, NOVEMBER 18TH, 1949

from 8 p.m. to 1 a.m.

with

Joe Loss and his Broadcasting Orchestra

and

The Billy Webb Quartet

Tickets 1 guinea each, inclusive.

Licensed Refreshments.   Dress Formal.

A ticket for the Joe Loss event in Studley, with the reverse showing autographs from Joe Loss and other members of the Orchestra.

using it. Understandably, especially with our heavy footwear! However, when leaving for the dance I was coerced into coming down the staircase. I was very reluctant and didn't enjoy it.

With the news of the disbandment at the end of 1950, a party was arranged at the hostel with a local reporter and photographer invited. I was interviewed, having served over seven years. We also had an invitation to a formal dress dance at the Shire Hall, Warwick.

I now had to plan a new life, always difficult! I could get help because of long service, to apply for a small holding, so with another long serving friend we considered the prospect of such an enterprise. Australia beckoned and won with the offer of a £10 passage to emigrate with a clause to stay for two years or repay the balance of the fare. Three of us decided to go, so we were busy with preparations, which helped to ease the goodbyes to families and friends and overcome our emotions on leaving the Land Army.

Appendix

Life after the WLA

A society was formed in 1964, entitled the British Women's Land Army Society. This continued until October 2005. Many events were arranged and reported in a monthly magazine. These included reunions, parades and Buckingham Palace garden parties. Also the Unveiling Ceremony of a Memorial to the Women of World War II, held in Whitehall on 9th July 2005. Our last reunion was on the 12th May 2001, at the Grand Hotel in Birmingham. There was a large audience, coming from all parts of the country. The following poem was read out:

THE FINAL REUNION 12 MAY 2001
(Read out at the reunion)

Sadly our final reunion is on the 12th of May
Sending for my ticket I am filled with dismay
I just couldn't get it out of my head
Right up to the time of going to bed
Then suddenly in the dead of night
This figure appeared in a great shaft of light
Saying, *Your Country Needs You*: I said, of course
I will comply
Then next thing, I'm speeding through the sky!
I landed as elegantly as a bird
Twas then I spotted this huge herd
They needed to be milked right away
I was suitably dressed so no delay
I was so energetic and my sight so clear
No arthritic hands, I could even hear!
I finished milking, everything was spick and span
Still not understanding how it all began
Then the figure appeared waving a Union Jack
Saying, come along the Queen Mother has made us a snack
She really was on her mettle
Already boiling the kettle
Prince Charles smiled and beckoned to me
The Queen won't be long she's making the tea
It was a dream no doubt you've guessed
But reliving those days I was quite impressed
At this final reunion at Birmingham Grand
We take pride and reminisce our life on the land
To the ceremony of the Flag our allegiance we pay
Renewing acquaintances, it will be a great day.

Nancy Cooper

Cover from programme of the final reunion in 2001.

In the gracious presence of Her Majesty The Queen

1980~2005
**NATIONAL
HERITAGE
MEMORIAL
FUND**

The Right Honourable Baroness Boothroyd of Sandwell PC and the Trustees of the
Memorial to the Women of World War II Charity extend an invitation to

MRS NANCY COOPER

to attend the Unveiling Ceremony of the Memorial to the Women of World War II
to be held in Whitehall on Saturday 9th July 2005 at 3pm and then to the Reception after the
Unveiling in the Pillared Hall of the Ministry of Defence just off Whitehall

This Invitation is Not Transferable

Guests must be seated by 2.30pm   **PLEASE SEE OVER**   RSVP: as shown on the RSVP card enclosed

*Invitation for the Unveiling
Ceremony of the Memorial to the
Women of World War II, 2005.*

*Betty Boothroyd attending the
Unveiling Ceremony.*

*The Queen attending the
Unveiling Ceremony.*

In 2008 the author was awarded a badge and it was presented at Moreton Morrell Agricultural College. The photograph shows the author (right) along with Mrs Margaret Simmons née Brown (left). Mrs Simmons was the author's forewoman at Park Hall, Salford Priors.

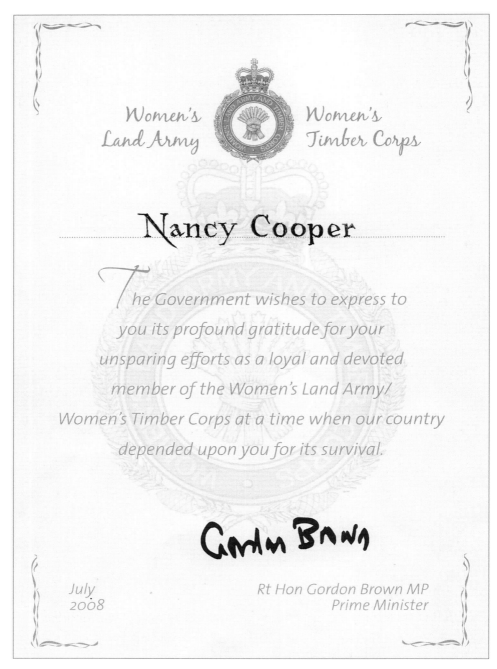

Women's Land Army

Women's Timber Corps

Nancy Cooper

The Government wishes to express to you its profound gratitude for your unsparing efforts as a loyal and devoted member of the Women's Land Army/ Women's Timber Corps at a time when our country depended upon you for its survival.

Gordon Brown

July
2008

*Rt Hon Gordon Brown MP
Prime Minister*

Letter of appreciation to the Women's Land Army from Gordon Brown.

I wrote thanking Gordon Brown (Prime Minister) and also took the opportunity to send the poem below. My husband served in Bomber Command and they were never awarded a medal. He didn't protest but many people did! All he would say was that he lost all his friends. However, my poem was passed to Headquarters Air Command and they replied with regret that it was too late.

A badge presented to the Bevin Boys and the WLA
Is very much appreciated, but may I say
Everyone who lived through wartime Britain
Suffered wartime consequences and were smitten
We were very much appreciated in our youth with so much to give
Vulnerable now in old age, by some it is resented we still live!
We fought with pride for "This England" it was worth fighting for
But today's values do not impress me and we fight a different war!
I mourn for all the lost lives that created so much pain
Their sacrifice for a better world, was it all in vain?
Next in line for an award will be the boys in blue
Namely Bomber Command who sacrificed their lives for me and you
Some never came down to earth they were just blasted away
A sacrifice intended to keep the enemy at bay
But those heroes were condemned for the task they were sent to do
They were never revered like the heroes, namely 'The Few'.
Night after night they were sent out with the knowledge they may not
    return
Those dedicated young men were blamed for desecration, no medal
    did they earn!
Their mission, death and destruction, sent by the powers that be
Was the same for all airmen, even the enemy.
Over 55,000 lost their lives, let's pay them a tribute to get their sacrifices
    revived
Award a medal to the heroes, those fortunate ones that survived.

Nancy Cooper

The author and her husband Joe after a street parade in Stratford upon Avon.

Joe's medals.

THE WOMEN'S LAND ARMY

We worked hard during wartime to help feed the nation
Producing food was a great salvation
In a natural environment we thrived and were fit
Some jobs seemed impossible but we tackled them with grit!
Expense is not necessary to commemorate our name,
But to forget us completely would be a great shame.

Nancy Cooper

I wrote the above poem after visiting the National Arboretum in 2010 and being unable to find a memorial for the WLA. I wrote to DEFRA and they confirmed that there wasn't one or for the Home Guard! I hope the Home Guard have finally been rewarded with a memorial after all their hard work and dedication! I was unaware that about the same time funding was being started by Staffordshire Branch of the Women's Food and Farming Union. On the 21st October 2014 a beautiful sculpture was presented and unveiled by HRH the Countess of Wessex. We owe so much to all the volunteers, thank you. We had to wait 64 years and so many Land Girls have departed, they would have been very proud.

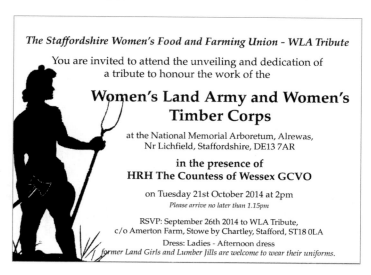

The Staffordshire Women's Food and Farming Union - WLA Tribute

You are invited to attend the unveiling and dedication of
a tribute to honour the work of the

Women's Land Army and Women's Timber Corps

at the National Memorial Arboretum, Alrewas,
Nr Lichfield, Staffordshire, DE13 7AR

in the presence of
HRH The Countess of Wessex GCVO

on Tuesday 21st October 2014 at 2pm
Please arrive no later than 1.15pm

RSVP: September 26th 2014 to WLA Tribute,
c/o Amerton Farm, Stowe by Chartley, Stafford, ST18 0LA

Dress: Ladies - Afternoon dress
former Land Girls and Lumber Jills are welcome to wear their uniforms.

HRH the Countess of Wessex at
the National Arboretum 2010.

The WLA memorial at
the National Arboretum.

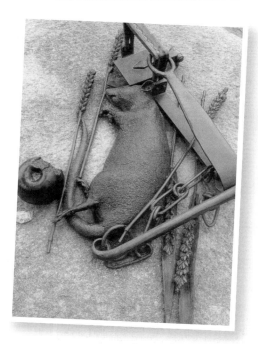

Even a rat features
on the memorial!

On the left the author's friend
Barbara Barrow (ex WLA) who
had come over from Australia.

The author celebrates a special birthday with a very special cake.

The cake was complete with Women's Land Army Cap Badge.

The author in front of the WLA memorial at the National Arboretum.